THE CRANE WIFE

THE CRANE WIFE

RETOLD BY *Odds Bodkin*

ILLUSTRATED BY *Gennady Spirin*

GULLIVER BOOKS

HARCOURT BRACE & COMPANY

San Diego   New York   London

The Crane Wife is one of Japan's best-known and most-loved folktales. It first spoke to me when a student offered her version of it in one of my graduate classes. I hope my version is close enough to those of the Japanese storytellers who first told it to do them honor. —O. B.

Special thanks to Akiko and Martin Collcutt, Kiyoko and Ty Heineken, and Ann Beneduce for their help in finding visual references from medieval Japan. —G. S.

Library of Congress Cataloging-in-Publication Data
Bodkin, Odds.
The crane wife/retold by Odds Bodkin; illustrated by Gennady Spirin.
p. cm.
"Gulliver Books."
Summary: A retelling of the traditional Japanese tale about a poor sail maker who gains a beautiful but mysterious wife skilled at weaving magical sails.
ISBN 0-15-201407-1
ISBN 0-8172-5767-5 (Library binding)
[1. Folklore—Japan.] I. Spirin, Gennadiĭ, ill. II. Title.
PZ8.1.B58835Cr 1998
398.2'0952'0452832—dc21 96-35488

F E D C B

Printed in Singapore

The illustrations in this book were done in watercolor and gouache on Arches paper.
The display type was hand lettered by John Stevens.
The text type was set in Granjon.
Color separations by Singapore Sang Choy Color Separation Pte Ltd
Printed and bound by Tien Wah Press, Singapore
This book was printed on totally chlorine-free Nymolla Matte Art paper.
Production supervision by Stanley Redfern and Pascha Gerlinger
Designed by Kaelin Chappell

For my beloved wife, Miguelina—
may she never fly away

—O. B.

For Ilya and Emily

—G. S.

Once, in ancient Japan, there lived a lonely sail maker named Osamu. Osamu's house was built high above the sea, on a hilltop. From where he sat weaving his sails, Osamu could see the green salt marsh below, dotted with white cranes. As he pulled the warp and weft of his sail fabric together, he would often think to himself, *How beautiful the cranes*

are. Of all the birds, they are the most like sails. It is as if the wind is held in their wings.

All his life Osamu had wished for a wife to comfort his lonely hours at the loom. But with one rice steamer, one pot for making tea, and little else, he knew his chances of finding a wife to live with him were small.

Autumn came, the season of storms. Red leaves fell on the dark wood of his porch. One night, as the winds howled, Osamu heard something strike his door. Curious, he looked out. There lay a great crane, stunned and still.

"Oh, poor bird!" he cried, kneeling. Osamu carefully folded the crane's crumpled wings and carried it inside. How light it was! So delicate! Amazed, he warmed the beautiful creature by his fire, caressing its wings. Soon its black, shining eyes opened.

For three days Osamu nursed the crane back to health. Then he watched it soar away.

Time passed and one night a great storm blew in from the sea. Through the sound of the pelting rain, Osamu heard a knocking on his door.

"Who is there?" called Osamu, peering out. A beautiful young woman gazed up at him, her black eyes shining.

"Who are you?" gasped Osamu.

"Help me!" cried the young woman, shivering in her wet garments.

"Oh, forgive me. Please come in." Osamu bowed and stared as she stepped inside. Never in all his life had he stood close to so beautiful a young woman.

Osamu served the young woman tea and rice, and a little bit of the precious fish given to him by the fishermen in the harbor. Gradually she stopped shivering. They knelt across from each other. The lamp flame flickered. Finally he found words. How had she come to him in the storm? Where was her family? Where was her home? Osamu asked her many questions, but all the young woman would tell him was that her name was Yukiko.

Time passed. Frost covered the black twigs outside Osamu's window, and still Yukiko had not left. It was beyond Osamu's wildest hope to think that she might stay. He was afraid to ask her to marry him. He had so little. Yet, as the days passed, a love grew between them. With no words spoken, Yukiko became his wife.

But Osamu was still just a poor sail maker. And it came to a time in the little house above the marsh when there was not enough food for the two of them to eat.

Yukiko saw this. She came to him one day and said, "Husband, I will weave you a magic sail that you may take and sell in the village below."

"You can weave a magic sail?"

She pulled the dressing screen across the room, hiding his loom, which sat near the window. "Yes, but you must promise never to look at me as I work," she said.

"Why?" Osamu asked.

"Promise me," Yukiko insisted.

And Osamu promised.

Yukiko began to work. Osamu could hear the shuttle sliding and the loom rocking. Hours passed. Night fell. Osamu slept. At dawn, Yukiko was still working behind the screen.

When at last she appeared, Yukiko looked very tired. *That's natural,* Osamu thought. *She has worked all night.* But when Yukiko placed the sail in his arms, Osamu forgot everything. Though immensely strong, the sail weighed nearly nothing at all. A sound like faraway whispering lifted from the folds. Osamu put his ear to the sail. His eyes went wide. Yukiko had woven in the wind!

Osamu ran to the harbor with the magic sail, showed it to all, and was paid enough gold to live for half a year! Overjoyed, he ran home. Yukiko smiled.

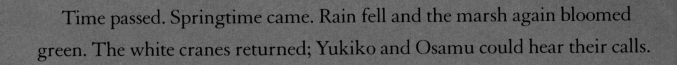

Time passed. Springtime came. Rain fell and the marsh again bloomed green. The white cranes returned; Yukiko and Osamu could hear their calls.

It was in late spring that the gold ran out. Once again Osamu and Yukiko grew hungry. Osamu said, "Yukiko, you should weave another magic sail."

"Oh, husband, I cannot," she replied. "It takes all that I am to weave such sails. I am afraid to weave another!"

"But, wife, please! One more! I will never ask again!"

Yukiko loved him.

"Do not watch me then," she said. And she disappeared behind the screen.

A full day passed.

"Yukiko!" Osamu called. "Do you want water? Do you want rice?" The only answer was the sound of the loom rocking.

At the end of two days, Yukiko emerged exhausted, holding a second sail. More beautiful than the first, it too held the wind.

Thinking only of gold, Osamu ran to the village and sold the magic sail. Everyone talked of Osamu's skill, for he told no one it was Yukiko who had made the sails. Again he was paid enough gold to last six long months.

Time passed. Autumn returned, the season of storms. The cranes in the marsh grew restless; their feathers ruffled in the bending grasses and flying leaves.

One day Osamu was visiting the village when a great trading ship docked in the harbor. From it strode a tall captain, a wealthy trader. The captain questioned the fishermen in the harbor, and they all pointed to Osamu.

"I have sailed a great distance to find you, Osamu," said the captain. "I want you to weave a magic sail for my ship."

Osamu thought of Yukiko and of the promise he had made. "I cannot," he replied. "The two I made are the only two I shall ever make."

The captain laughed. "Make me a sail, Osamu, and I will pay you a lifetime's gold. You shall never work again!"

A lifetime's gold, thought Osamu. *Imagine!*

Home he ran. "Yukiko!" he called. "There is a man in the harbor who will give us a lifetime's gold if"—he stopped in the door—"if you will weave one more sail."

Fear swept across Yukiko's face. "Osamu, no! I am afraid!"

"Yukiko! A lifetime's gold! Don't you see? We will never want for tea or rice again."

"But these sails, they take so much from me," she pleaded. "It is my very self they take."

Osamu frowned at Yukiko. "I am your husband!" he said, his voice growing loud. "I command you!"

Yukiko began to weep. "Very well," she said, trembling, "but promise you will not look at me."

"I promise! Now go! Make my sail!"

Yukiko pulled the screen before the loom and disappeared. Outside Osamu paced his porch. He could see the ship at anchor in the harbor, waiting. A day passed. Then another. Still Yukiko worked. A third day dawned. Never had she worked so long.

What is she doing? Osamu wondered.

"Yukiko!" he called. "Do you want water? Do you want rice?" But she gave no answer.

Why, wondered Osamu, should only Yukiko know how to weave magic sails? Why could he not learn the secret of weaving in the wind? Then he could make many magic sails! And he could save Yukiko the work she did not wish to do.

Osamu could hear the shuttle sliding and the loom rocking. "Yukiko! Answer me!"

Unable to contain himself, Osamu ran around the screen. A long beak swung toward him. Sad black eyes gleamed at him. There stood the crane he had saved in the storm!

"Yukiko!"

The bird was weaving its white feathers into the sail on the loom. Filled with sea wind, the feathers were trembling.

"Yukiko!" Osamu cried. But the only answer his crane wife could give was a soft, strange sound, like a cat purring in bamboo reeds. Then Yukiko spread her tattered wings, lifting herself through the window and into the sky.

Never again did Osamu see her. He wove simple sails for the rest of his years, there at his window, gazing at the marsh and the white cranes. And each autumn, in the season of storms, he waited for a knock on his door.